To my husband Cristian,
who inspires me daily to love with
all my heart .

Hey there lovers!

There are no rules to using this book. It's meant to be fun so you can skip to your favourite activities and flip back and forth.

The writing prompts and activities in this book are designed to help you and your partner connect. Most importantly, it's aimed to bring play and fun into your relationship.

No matter how long you've been together, there's always more to learn. Just when you think you've run out of date ideas, you might be inspired to find more.

Use these activities as a starting point to deepen your love and have fun doing it.

I'd love to see how your activities go. Tag me on Instagram @30everafter or leave me a note at iona@30everafter.com.

Writing prompt

When was the
last time we partied like it was 1999?

Lover A:

_____

_____

_____

_____

_____

Lover B:

_____

_____

_____

_____

_____

Draw It

Remember our first date?

Draw it in a comic.

Lover A

Draw It

Remember our first date?

Draw it in a comic.

Lover B

Pop Quiz ?

Give yourself a point for each question you get right.

1. What's your partner's favourite colour?

2. What's your partner's dream car?

3. Does your partner have any hidden talents?

4. What's your partner's favourite nickname for you?

5. When was the last time your partner cried?

6. What's your partner's favourite past time?

7. How would your partner describe you?

8. What's your partner's favourite song?

9. What annoys your partner most?

10. What dish could your partner eat every single day?

11. What's your partner's favourite song?

12. What makes your partner laugh out loud?

13. What's relaxing to your partner?

14. What's your partner's idea of the perfect day?

15. Which part of your body does your partner love the most?

Moments

List three moments where you thought
'I love her/him'.

Lover A:

_____

_____

_____

_____

Lover B:

_____

_____

_____

_____

Activity

Watch your partner doing something they love from afar.

In one of Ester Perel's Ted Talks, she shares when partners find the other the most attractive. It's when one is observing them from a distance. Watch your partner play a sports match if they love sports. Go to a party and go mingle from opposite sides of the room. Have them watch you dance.

Writing prompt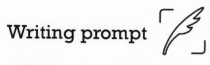

Finish the sentence.
I never thought we'd be...

Lover A:

_____

_____

_____

_____

_____

Lover B:

_____

_____

_____

_____

_____

Draw It

If your partner was a super hero.
What would he/she look like?

Partner's superhero name:

Super power:

Draw It

If your partner was a super hero. What would he/she look like?

Partner's superhero name:

Super power:

Pop Quiz ?

Give yourself a point for each question you get right.

1. What's your partner's favourite emoji?

2. Name the catch phrase your partner always uses

3. What's your partner's biggest pet peeve?

4. Who was your partner's first crush?

5. Does your partner like public displays of affection?

6. What's one thing that would make your partner's day?

7. What's one thing your partner can't get enough of?

8. What's your partner's karaoke tune?

9. Who does your partner admire the most?

10. Is your partner more like dad or mom?

11. What would make your partner happy today?

12. What's your partner's least favourite colour?

13. Did your partner have a childhood pet?

14. What's one cause your partner is most passionate about?

15. What's one article of clothing your partner will never ever throw away?

Moments

Reflect on an occasion you loved sharing with your partner

Lover A:

_____

_____

_____

_____

_____

Lover B:

_____

_____

_____

_____

_____

Activity
The Ha Ha game

Look each other in the eye. Have one person
go first to start the game. Whisper 'ha ha'
without laughing. The next person repeats 'ha
ha' but a little louder. Take turns until one
person burts into laughter. The person who
can refrain from laughing wins!

Writing prompt

Write down your favourite pet names for your partner.

Lover A:

_____

_____

_____

_____

_____

_____

_____

_____

Writing prompt

Write down your favourite pet names for your partner.

Lover B:

_____

_____

_____

_____

_____

_____

_____

_____

Draw It
The nine box: Partner A

Share nine things that describe who you are

The car that best describes you	One piece of article that represents you	Your favourite music album
A dish you can eat every day	People you love	A decade you'd live in
Biggest fear	Which animal would you be?	Four people you'd like to invite to dinner

Draw It
The nine box: Partner A

Share nine things that describe who you are

Draw It
The nine box: Partner B

Share nine things that describe who you are

The car that best describes you	One piece of article that represents you	Your favourite music album
A dish you can eat every day	People you love	A decade you'd live in
Biggest fear	Which animal would you be?	Four people you'd like to invite to dinner

Draw It
The nine box: Partner B

Share nine things that describe who you are

Solve it

Race to solve the word scramble.
Best two out of three

levantine

ahrodiIspac

olevr

Quotables

Things your partner has said...

Partner A

Funniest thing my partner has ever said:

_____

_____

_____

Most memorable thing your partner
has ever said:

_____

_____

_____

Quotables

Things your partner has said...
Partner B

Funniest thing my partner has ever said:

_____

_____

_____

**Most memorable thing your partner
has ever said:**

_____

_____

_____

Draw It

Draw a portrait of your partner (naked_)

Draw It

Draw a portrait of your partner (naked_)

Couples Pictionary

Take a few sheets of paper.
Take turns writing facts about your marriage like your favourite takeaway place, where you first met, your wedding date…etc. Have one person draw a slip of paper and draw it for the other person to guess.

Writing prompt

Write down your favourite pet names for your partner.

Lover A:

_____

_____

_____

_____

_____

_____

_____

_____

Writing prompt

Write down your favourite pet names for your partner.

Lover B:

_____

_____

_____

_____

_____

_____

_____

_____

Draw It.
Write your partner a love note…in emojis.
Partner A

Draw It.
Write your partner a love note…in emojis.
Partner B

Real Talk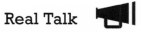
So many ways to love you...
List 10 things your partner can do to woo you
Partner A

_____

_____

_____

_____

_____

_____

_____

_____

_____

_____

Real Talk
So many ways to love you...
List 10 things your partner can do to woo you
Partner B

_____

_____

_____

_____

_____

_____

_____

_____

_____

_____

Romantic Tic Tac Toe

It's just like the game you know but better. One
person will have x's. The other will have o's. Place
either an x or o in each box and follow the
instructions.

Kiss your partner on the lips	Give your partner a 5 min massage	Serenade your partner
Cuddle your partner for one minute	Give your partner a compliment	Tell your partner you love them
Kiss your partner on the cheek	Tell your partner something they don't already know about you	Make your partner a quick snack

Romantic Tic Tac Toe

Your Scorecard

The Apple Game

Grab an apple or orange and pass it to your partner without using your hands. If you drop it, start over. Too easy? Add another apple or orange into the mix.

Draw It.

Map out your dream home. Draw the floor plan.

Partner A

Draw It.
Map out your dream home. Draw the floor plan.
Partner B

Real Talk 📣

Fill in the blanks

Partner A

A time when I felt the most proud of you...

When you passed your Boards

You made me so happy when...

you SAID Alright, Let's do this

I love you the most when...

I WAKE UP next to you

I felt so proud to call you mine when...

Always !!!

The first time I knew I still love you was...

When I saw you At Macondo for mimi's BDAY

Real Talk 📢
Fill in the blanks
Partner B

A time when I felt the most proud of you...

when I dropped you off at your first deployment.

You made me so happy when...

you never went back home.

I love you the most when...

you surprise me / are thoughtful

I felt so proud to call you mine when...

I hear someone say Lt. Antelo

The first time I knew I love you was...

when I wrote Mrs. Antelo all over my FIU agenda

Writing prompt

Come up with your most creative date ideas

Lover A:

_____

_____

_____

_____

_____

_____

_____

_____

_____

Writing prompt

Come up with your most creative date ideas

Lover B:

_____

_____

_____

_____

_____

_____

_____

_____

The Love Memory Game

Re-create the tiles on this page and the next (or just cut them from this page). Match two cards together and follow the instructions.

Kiss Me	Kiss Me	Hug Me
Hug Me	5 minute massage	5 minute massage
Show me some love	Show me some love	xoxo

The Love Memory Game

Re-create the tiles below or just cut them from this page. Match two cards together and follow the instructions.

xoxo	Truth or Dare	Truth or Dare
Dance	Dance	Cuddle Me
Cuddle Me	Get Naked	Get Naked

Love Memory Game

Your Scorecard

Love Notes

Write your partner love notes, cut them out into strips and put them in a glass jar for him/her to read for the next three days.

Partner A

Love Notes

Write your partner love notes, cut them out into
strips and put them in a glass jar for him/her to read
for the next three days.

Partner B

Writing prompt

Things we should put on our bucket list

Lover A:

_____

_____

_____

_____

_____

_____

_____

_____

_____

Writing prompt

Things we should put on our bucket list

Lover B:

_____

_____

_____

_____

_____

_____

_____

_____

Writing prompt

Brag about your partner. Fill in the blanks.

Love A:

[Insert name] is

_____.

she/he has a super secret power that
lets you _____. She/He
uses this super power for good along
with her/his other talents

_____, _____ and
_____. I love her/him because

_____.

Writing prompt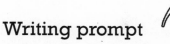

Brag about your partner. Fill in the blanks.

Love B:

[Insert name] is

_____.

she/he has a super secret power that

lets you _____. She/He

uses this super power for good along

with her/his other talents

_____, _____ and

_____. I love her/him because

_____.

Draw It

Draw your favourite memory and have the other person guess it.

Partner A

Draw It

Draw your favourite memory and have the other person guess it.

Partner B

Writing prompt

List 10 things you've learned about
relationships

Lover A:

_____

_____

_____

_____

_____

_____

_____

_____

_____

Writing prompt

List 10 things you've learned about

relationships

Lover B:

_____

_____

_____

_____

_____

_____

_____

_____

Romantic Tic Tac Toe

It's just like the game you know but better. One person will have x's. The other will have o's. Place either an x or o in each box and follow the instructions.

Tell your partner a secret	Truth or Dare	Sing a duet
Have a tickle fight	Give your partner a sensual kiss	Have a staring contest
Kiss your partner on the cheek	Give your partner a quick 5 minute massage	Give your partner a hug

Romantic Tic Tac Toe

Your Scorecard

Choose your own love adventure

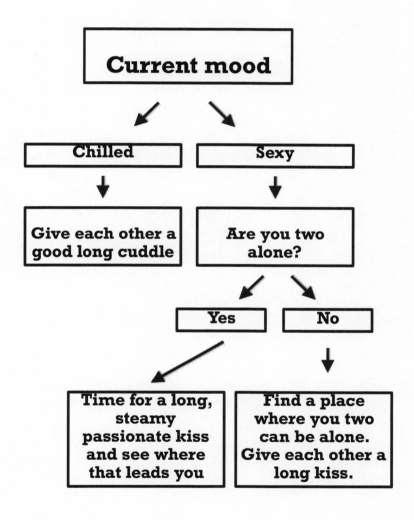

Current mood

Chilled

Sexy

Give each other a good long cuddle

Are you two alone?

Yes

No

Time for a long, steamy passionate kiss and see where that leads you

Find a place where you two can be alone. Give each other a long kiss.

Draw It

Draw what your life looks like in 5 years
Partner A

Draw It

Draw what your life looks like in 5 years
Partner B

Writing prompt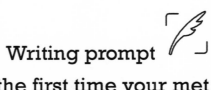

Describe the first time your met your partner

Lover A:

_____

_____

_____

_____

_____

_____

_____

_____

_____

Writing prompt

Describe the first time your met your partner

Lover B:

_____

_____

_____

_____

_____

_____

_____

_____

_____

Real Talk 📢

Fill in the blanks
Partner A

I feel the most scared when...

_____

Things that keep me up at night are...

_____

I'm vulnerable when...

_____

When it comes to confrontation, I...

_____

What calms me most...

_____

Real Talk

Fill in the blanks

Partner B

I feel the most scared when...

_____

Things that keep me up at night are...

_____

I'm vulnerable when...

_____

When it comes to confrontation, I...

_____

What calms me most...

_____

Writing prompt

When was the last time you got really excited about something?

Lover A:

_____

_____

_____

_____

_____

_____

_____

_____

Writing prompt

When was the last time you got really excited about something?

Lover B:

_____

_____

_____

_____

_____

_____

_____

_____

_____

Love Notes

Write your partner ten love notes and put them in a
jar. Open one each day.

Love Notes

Write your partner ten love notes and put them in a jar. Open one each day.

Love Notes

Write your partner ten love notes and put them in a
jar. Open one each day.

Love Notes

Write your partner ten love notes and put them in a
jar. Open one each day.

Date Night Ideas

Come up with as many date ideas as you can.

_____

_____

_____

_____

_____

_____

_____

_____

Date Night Ideas

Come up with as many date ideas as you can.

_____

_____

_____

_____

_____

_____

_____

_____

_____

Date Night Ideas

Come up with as many date ideas as you can.

_____

_____

_____

_____

_____

_____

_____

_____

Date Night Ideas

Come up with as many date ideas as you can.

_____

_____

_____

_____

_____

_____

_____

_____

Date Night Ideas

Come up with as many date ideas as you can.

_____

_____

_____

_____

_____

_____

_____

_____

Date Night Ideas

Come up with as many date ideas as you can.

_____

_____

_____

_____

_____

_____

_____

_____

_____

Date Night Ideas

Come up with as many date ideas as
you can.

_____

_____

_____

_____

_____

_____

_____

_____

Date Night Ideas

Come up with as many date ideas as
you can.

_____

_____

_____

_____

_____

_____

_____

_____

Date Night Ideas

Come up with as many date ideas as you can.

_____

_____

_____

_____

_____

_____

_____

_____

Date Night Ideas

Come up with as many date ideas as
you can.

_____

_____

_____

_____

_____

_____

_____

_____

Date Night Ideas

Come up with as many date ideas as
you can.

_____

_____

_____

_____

_____

_____

_____

_____

Reflection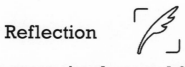

List three things you've learned from finishing this activity book

Lover A:

_____

_____

_____

_____

Lover B:

_____

_____

_____

_____

Thank you!

How did you do?

I'd love your feedback on volume 2 of this activity book. Tag me on Instagram @30everafter or leave me a note at iona@30everafter.com.

73271317R00064

Made in the USA
Columbia, SC
03 September 2019